THE FACTS ABOUT
Asthma

Claire Llewellyn

Thameside Press

Distributed in the United States by
Smart Apple Media
1980 Lookout Drive
North Mankato, MN 56003

Text by Claire Llewellyn
Illustration by Tom Connell

Editor: Russell McLean
Designer: Helen James
Picture researcher: Frances Vargo
Medical consultant: Helen Harris, practice nurse (asthma), Hertfordshire, England

Thanks to Pat Georgette and Trudy Watson of the American Lung Association for
help with the U.S. edition.

The author and publishers would like to thank Alison, Christopher, Donna, Hannah,
Jessica, Lucy, and Martin for their help in preparing this book.

Printed in China

9 8 7 6 5 4 3 2 1

Library of Congress Cataloging-in-Publication Data

Llewellyn, Claire.
    Asthma / written by Claire Llewellyn.
        p. cm. -- (The facts about ...)
    Includes index.
    ISBN 1-929298-95-1
        1. Asthma--Juvenile literature. 2. Asthma in children--Juvenile literature. [1. Asthma.
    2. Diseases.] I. Title. II. Facts about (Mankato, Minn.)

    RC591 .L565 2001
    616.2'38--dc21
                                                                          2001027261

Picture acknowledgements:
Belitha Press: David Towersey 3r, 14t, 18–19. Corbis: Nathan Benn 16t; Pablo Corral 25b; Duomo
28b; Ed Eckstein 22b; Owen Franken 22t; Jeffry W. Myers 25t; Keren Su 23t. Eye Ubiquitous:
Yiorgos Nikiteas 6b; Sue Passmore 5b; Paul Seheult 8t. Sally & Richard Greenhill: Sally Greenhill 7b,
20t. Medipics: cover bl, 6t; Dan McCoy/Rainbow 23b. Photofusion: Crispin Hughes 4b; Ute Klaphake
26t; Clarissa Leahy 27b; Julia Martin 29b; David Montford cover background & cover bc, 11b, 29t.
Rex Features: 10b, 17t, 28t; Jonathon Buckmaster 3c, 9b; Florence Durand 8b; Steve Lyne 24; John
Powell 27t; Skyline Features 16b. Science Photo Library: BSIP Laurent/Bouhier 4t; Dr Jeremy Burgess
11t; Mark Clarke 12t&b, 14b, 17b; Alain Dex/Publiphoto Diffusion 15t; James King-Holmes 13;
K.H. Kjeldsen cover br, 10t; Dr P. Marazzi 20b; David Parker 9t; D. Phillips 3l, 21t; Garry Watson 1,
15b. David Towersey: 5t, 21b, 26b.

Contents

What is asthma?   4

What happens inside?   6

Who has asthma?   8

What starts asthma?   10

An asthma attack   12

Treating asthma   14

Controlling asthma   16

The asthma nurse   18

Eczema and asthma   20

A history of asthma   22

Asthma at school   24

Asthma at home   26

Questions people ask   28

Glossary and useful organizations   30

Index   32

Words in **bold** are explained
in the glossary on page 30

What is asthma?

Asthma is a condition that affects people's breathing. Breathing comfortably is something most of us never have to think about. But if you have asthma, there are times when it is very difficult to breathe.

The signs of asthma
You can't always tell that someone has asthma, but sometimes there are obvious signs. These signs are known as **symptoms**.

You can't tell just by looking who has asthma.

A tight feeling in the chest is one of the symptoms of asthma.

Many people have to live with asthma. This is how some of them describe their symptoms:

*"It feels like someone is standing on my **lungs**."*

"My chest feels tight. It's hard for me to breathe."

"My breathing is squeaky."

"I get tired very quickly."

The four symptoms of asthma

- Coughing, often worse at night or during exercise.
- **Wheezing**, a whistling noise in the chest.
- Becoming short of breath.
- A tight feeling in the chest.

Severe asthma symptoms make it difficult to breathe.

An asthma attack

From time to time, the symptoms of a person with asthma become very severe. They have to fight for their breath, end up breathing too quickly, and feel as though they are going to suffocate. This is known as an asthma attack, and it can be very frightening.

"It's really horrible. It feels like I've got glue in my lungs and a ton of bricks on my chest."

MARTIN, AGE 11

Living with asthma

Everybody's asthma is different. Some people have very mild asthma, with little more than the occasional cough or wheeze. For others, the symptoms are more severe and may affect their sleep and daily life.

Most of us never have to think about breathing. People with asthma do.

What happens inside?

Asthma is a kind of **allergy**, a reaction by the body to something it meets that is harmless to most people. Some allergies make you sneeze or itch. Asthma makes it hard to breathe.

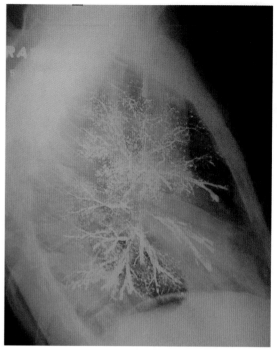

This x-ray reveals the thousands of tiny airways inside the lungs.

Inside the lungs

Every time you breathe in, air is sucked into your **windpipe** and down into your lungs through tubes called **airways,** or **bronchioles.** The airways become smaller and smaller as they go deeper into the lungs, until they are really tiny.

Inside the airways

Each airway has a lining that is ringed by muscles. The lining makes a thick, sticky liquid called **mucus.** Mucus protects the lungs by warming the air we breathe in and trapping any tiny **particles** it contains.

Every breath we take carries tiny substances deep into our lungs.

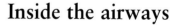

Irritated airways

The airways of people with asthma are almost always red and sore, or **inflamed**. Inflamed airways are easily irritated—sometimes by substances called **allergens** (such as smoke, pollen, or animal fur) and sometimes by other things, such as cold, dry air.

Meeting a trigger

Anything that irritates the airways is known as a **trigger**. When a person with asthma comes into contact with one of their triggers, the muscles around the airways tighten.

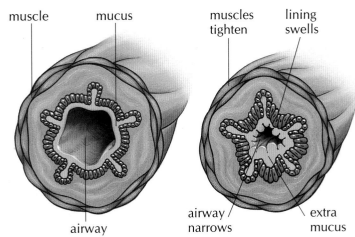

muscle mucus muscles tighten lining swells

airway airway narrows extra mucus

A healthy airway (left) is much wider than the airway of someone having an asthma attack (right).

The lining swells and makes too much mucus. All these things make the airways narrower, and bring on the symptoms of asthma: coughing, breathlessness, and wheezing.

Long-term effects

Most people can control their asthma with medicine. If asthma is not treated, it can cause long-term damage to the lungs. Over time, the inflamed linings of the airways grow thicker and become scarred, and the tiny tubes are blocked by mucus. This leads to more frequent and severe asthma attacks.

If you have asthma, coming into contact with a trigger can make you cough.

Who has asthma?

People can develop asthma at any time, from childhood to old age. Most new cases of asthma affect very young children, but now more and more adults and older people are getting asthma, too.

Several members of the same family often have asthma, eczema, or hayfever.

Children with asthma
Asthma usually starts in young children. Breathing difficulties and wheezing can begin at an early age, but a doctor may need a year or two to be sure the symptoms are really asthma. The condition often runs in families, so a child may inherit asthma from a parent.

Hayfever makes your eyes and nose run. It is closely related to asthma.

Close relations
Hayfever and **eczema** are closely related to asthma. In a single family you may find one person with asthma, one with hayfever, and another with eczema. Asthma symptoms often grow milder or disappear completely during the teenage years—although they may reappear in later life.

Asthma in adults

There are more and more new cases of asthma among adults. Some cases are triggered by air pollution. Others begin at work, where flour or grain, agricultural chemicals, spray paints, glues, wood dust, and rubber are all triggers. This kind of asthma is known as **occupational** asthma.

Spray-painting can trigger asthma in adults.

Older people

Older people get asthma, too. They are more likely to catch colds and chest infections, which are two major triggers. Unfortunately, many older people overlook their asthma. They think their breathlessness is just part of growing old.

Did you know?

- One child in seven is treated for the symptoms of asthma.
- About one in three children lose their symptoms by the time they are adults.
- In childhood, asthma is more common in boys. By the age of 18, it is more common in girls.
- Overall, about 5 to 7 per cent of Americans have asthma.

A growing problem

Asthma is increasing across all age groups. Most people with asthma live in the world's richest nations. Perhaps something in our lifestyle is to blame? Some scientists think that **immunizations**, which protect us from disease, leave our bodies more open to allergens.

Air pollution is a major trigger among children and adults.

What starts asthma?

Many ordinary things can trigger the symptoms of asthma. Everyone has their own particular triggers. It's important that people with asthma know what their triggers are, because then they can try to avoid them.

Colds and flu
Colds, flu, and chest infections are the most common asthma triggers. They are hard to avoid, especially in fall and winter, when asthma attacks reach their peak.

Cigarette smoke
Cigarette smoke has a sudden effect on people with asthma. As the smoke irritates their airways, they become breathless and start to cough.

Cigarette smoke often brings on the symptoms of asthma.

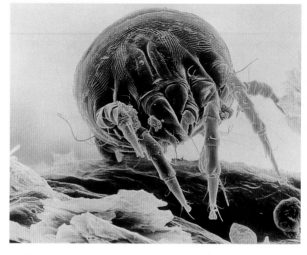

A house dust mite, pictured about 500 times bigger than real size.

Dust mites
House dust mites are a major trigger. These **microscopic** animals live in carpets, curtains, mattresses, pillows, and soft toys.

Air pollution
Air pollution from smoke, car fumes, gas fumes, spray paints, perfumes, and even felt-tip pens can all trigger the symptoms of asthma. So can poor air quality on hot summer days.

Exercise
Exercise makes most of us puff, and some people with asthma find it brings on their symptoms.

Smoking and asthma

- 85 per cent of the smoke from a lit cigarette goes straight into the air, where it is breathed in by other people.
- Smoke is a trigger for 8 out of 10 people with asthma.
- Teenagers who smoke are less likely to grow out of asthma than non-smokers.
- Children whose parents smoke are more than twice as likely to develop asthma symptoms.

Pollen is a common asthma trigger.

Pollen

Pollen grains can lodge inside the eyes, nose, and throat, making them irritated and inflamed.

Weather

Cold, dry air, and strong winds can all trigger asthma symptoms.

Medicines

Some common medicines, such as aspirin, can be a trigger.

Feelings

Being upset, worried, or very excited can bring on the symptoms of asthma. So can a laughing fit.

Mold and dampness

Microscopic **fungi** can bring on asthma. They grow indoors in damp kitchens and bathrooms, and outdoors in damp wood and piles of leaves.

Pets

Pets are bad news for some people with asthma. Their feathers, fur, saliva, and skin flakes are all triggers.

A furry friend? Many pets have a harmful effect on people with asthma.

An asthma attack

Gasping for breath, a pounding heart, and a feeling of suffocating are all symptoms of an asthma attack. Severe attacks are rare, but they can be very scary.

Out of the blue
If you have asthma, there are times when your symptoms suddenly grow worse—you cough, wheeze, and your chest feels tight. Soon you are gasping for breath. This is an asthma attack.

A severe asthma attack is exhausting and very frightening.

Some attacks are very severe. Breathing becomes more and more difficult, and each breath is shorter than the last. In the end, you are exhausted and almost suffocating. You need to go to the hospital—fast.

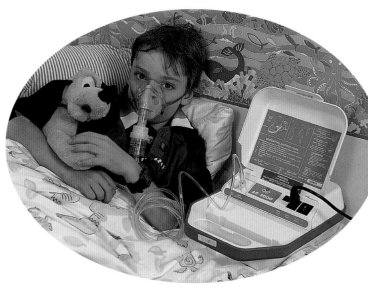

A nebulizer helps to get medicine deep into the lungs.

At the hospital
At the hospital's Emergency Room (ER), you are met by a nurse who checks your breathing, your pulse, and the oxygen in your blood. You may be given extra medicine through a machine called a **nebulizer**.

The nebulizer turns medicine into a fine mist that you can breathe deeply into the lungs. You may spend a few days in the hospital until you are breathing and sleeping normally, and feel well enough to go home.

Asthma can kill

People can die from an asthma attack, but this is extremely rare. Most people can prevent serious attacks by avoiding triggers and taking their medicine.

"When I have an asthma attack I can't stop coughing. It makes me very scared."

CHRISTOPHER, AGE 8

A short stay in the hospital helps people to recover after a severe asthma attack.

How to help in an asthma attack

- Find the person's "rescue med" (see page 14) and make sure they take it correctly.
- Stay calm and reassure them. Don't put your arm round them.
- Encourage them to breathe slowly and deeply.
- Help them to sit upright or lean forwards. Do not let them lie flat.
- Loosen tight clothing and offer them a drink of water.

Call 911 for an ambulance:

- If the medicine has not worked after five to ten minutes.
- If the person is very upset and unable to breathe properly.
- If the person is exhausted.

Make sure they take their inhaler every few minutes until the ambulance arrives.

Treating asthma

People who take their medicines carefully and regularly can control their asthma and its symptoms so well that most of the time no one will know there is anything wrong.

Inhalers may come in different colors, designs, and characters.

Twin treatments

Asthma is treated with two main types of medicines, called **relievers** and **controllers**. Each medicine works in a different way, but both need to be breathed deeply into the lungs. They both come in small packs called **inhalers** or puffers.

Relievers

Reliever medicines, or rescue meds, relieve the symptoms of asthma as soon as they appear. Relievers relax the muscles around the airways, making breathing easier. The medicine does not treat the **inflammation** in the airway itself. The most common rescue med is called albuterol.

A couple of puffs on a rescue med before exercising can stop symptoms appearing.

Did you know?

- Some inhalers contain 200 doses of medicine.
- Medicine can shoot out of an inhaler at 75 mph!

Instant relief

People with asthma carry their rescue med wherever they go. It is especially important during an asthma attack, because it can provide almost instant relief.

This disk inhaler is different from many puffers, because it does not use chemicals that damage the ozone layer.

Controllers

Controllers, or maintenance medications, calm the inflamed airways and stop them being irritated so easily. This helps to control the asthma and reduce the risk of an attack. Because the effect of the medicine builds up over time, you need to take it every day—even when you feel well. Instead of putting the inhaler straight into the mouth, it is often slotted into a large plastic container called a **spacer**.

How to use an inhaler

1 Click the inhaler to get a measured **dose**.
2 Suck in slowly. This gets the drug into the airways.
3 Hold your breath and count to ten.
4 Breathe out.

Young children may use a spacer to help them get more medication into their airways.

Controlling asthma

People can help control
their asthma by keeping a
diary, checking their lungs,
and avoiding their triggers.

A good diet helps us resist colds and flu.

Colds and flu
Resist colds and flu by eating plenty
of fresh fruit and vegetables.

Dust mites
Reduce the number of dust mites
by dusting and vacuuming daily,
and letting fresh air into rooms.
For more, see pages 26-27.

Cigarette smoke
Avoid smoky rooms if you can.

Cold air
Dress warmly. A scarf worn over
the face warms the air before it
is breathed in.

Air pollution
Avoid busy roads, especially during
rush hours.

Pets
Try to avoid furry or feathery pets
completely. If that's impossible, keep
pets out of the bedroom and wash
them and their bedding once a week.

*Wearing a scarf can prevent cold air
from irritating the airways.*

Yoga helps people to relax and stay calm.

Exercise

If exercise is their trigger, people with asthma should warm up gently and take their rescue med before they start. **Yoga** and other relaxation exercises can help people feel calmer.

Pollen

When the pollen count is high, close windows and avoid going outside.

Dampness

To reduce dampness at home, dry wet clothes outside, use lids on saucepans, and keep windows open.

Keep a diary

Some people with asthma find it hard to identify their triggers because the symptoms are delayed. Keeping a diary shows when they are free of symptoms and when their asthma is bad. The entries often reveal a pattern, which can help show a trigger.

Lung check

A **peak flow meter** is a plastic tube which measures how hard a person can blow air out of their lungs. The higher the score for the person's age and height, the better their asthma is being controlled. Marking the scores on a chart twice a day shows whether the asthma is getting worse, getting better, or staying the same. If the asthma is getting worse, the person may need to take extra medicine.

How to take a peak flow reading

1 Make sure the needle on the side of the meter is set to zero.
2 Take a deep breath and blow as hard as you can into the mouthpiece.
3 Write down your score.
4 Blow twice more. Write down each score.
5 Choose the highest of the three scores. Mark it on the chart.

The asthma nurse

Respiratory therapists and nurses work alongside doctors. They help and advise children and parents on how to keep asthma under control.

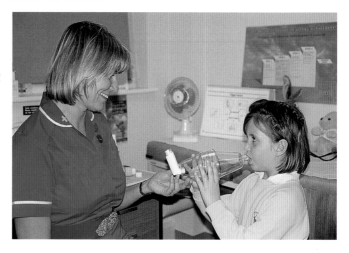

Helen asks each patient to show her how they use their inhaler.

A friendly face

Helen Roberts is a respiratory therapist in a clinic. Some people see her once a month, others two or three times a year. Helen helps them control their asthma. Each year in the U.S., there are over ten million visits to doctors' offices because of asthma. One-third of these visits are for patients under age 18.

Keeping a check

Helen makes a number of checks at each appointment. She looks at a patient's peak flow readings to see how their asthma has been. They may need to take more medicine, or perhaps a little less.

Then she checks that the patient is using their inhaler properly. It's easy to suck in too fast, or hold the breath for less than a count of ten. Helen also weighs and measures young children to make sure they are growing properly.

Helen weighs her young patients at each appointment.

Children at the clinic play games to practice sucking in their medicine.

Making it fun

Many young children find it hard to suck in their medicine. To give them extra practice, Helen plays games with them— such as sucking up candy with a straw. Putting a ping-pong ball inside their spacer makes medicine time more fun. Other children have problems blowing out. Fixing a pinwheel to their peak flow meter encourages them to blow out as hard as they can.

"Helen has helped me because she gave me my puffer and spacer. She gives me lots of stickers and lets me look through all the drawers. I like her very much."

CHRISTOPHER, AGE 8

Helping the family

Helen sees the parents of children with asthma, too. She reassures them that their child's asthma can be kept under control. She also meets the other children in the family to make sure they don't feel left out. Young patients need to build up a relationship with someone they trust, like Helen. In future years, they will come to the clinic without their parents and will be able to ask her for help and advice.

To make sure that no one feels left out, Helen meets all the children in a family.

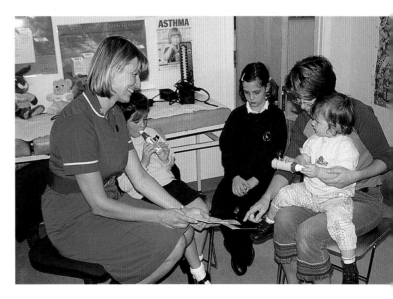

Eczema and asthma

Eczema is a skin condition related to asthma. Like asthma, it is caused by allergies, becomes worse with certain triggers, and is growing more common.

Taking a bath can be painful for children with eczema.

What is eczema?

Eczema is a skin condition in which patches of skin feel dry and itchy. In time, they become sore and may even crack open, blister, or **weep**.

Eczema is usually found on the face or neck, on the inside of elbows and wrists, or on the back of ankles and knees.

Types of eczema

There are two main kinds of eczema. One kind is caused by direct contact with a substance, such as a brand of laundry detergent or soap. The other kind, which is related to asthma, is caused by allergens such as pollen and animal fur.

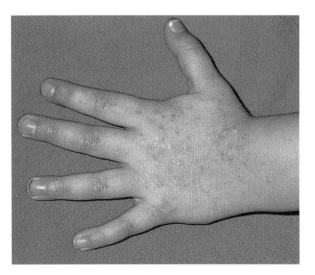

The eczema on this child's hand has been caused by an allergy to cats.

Pollen grains can cause eczema. These grains are 10,000 times bigger than their real size.

Who gets eczema?

Eczema often runs in families. Most children with eczema show the symptoms between the age of six months and two years. It is a difficult condition for them to handle. Their itchy skin keeps them awake at night, making them and their parents tired and irritable. There is no known cure for eczema, but fortunately most children grow out of it by the time they are teenagers.

Did you know?

- Eczema affects around one in eight children.
- More than half of all children with eczema develop asthma at some time in their lives.
- About nine out of ten children with eczema grow out of it by the time they are teenagers.

Treating eczema

Often, eczema can be controlled with skin creams and oils. These help to **moisturize** the skin, making it less dry and itchy. Adding oils to bath water helps, too. In severe cases of eczema, special creams treat the inflammation itself.

Skin creams can ease the symptoms of eczema.

How to cope with eczema

- Avoid furry and feathery pets.
- Try to reduce dust mites in the house (see pages 26-27).
- Wear cotton next to the skin.
- Keep the bedroom cool at night (eczema is worse when it's hot).
- Use light, cotton bed linen.
- Wear cotton gloves at night to avoid scratching.

A history of asthma

People have known about asthma since ancient times. After the first strange ideas for remedies, asthma treatments began to work. Now, as we learn more about asthma, who knows what the future may bring?

Chinese herbalists use plant remedies to treat asthma.

Ancient asthma
The symptoms of asthma were first written about in ancient Egypt over 3,500 years ago. The recommended remedy was camel and crocodile dung! Doctors in ancient China also treated asthma. They tried **acupuncture**, **meditation**, plant remedies, and yoga, which many people still use today.

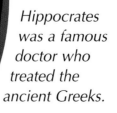

Hippocrates was a famous doctor who treated the ancient Greeks.

Poetry and wine
The word asthma comes from an ancient Greek word meaning "to breathe hard." It first appeared in about 800 B.C. in a long poem called the *Iliad*, by Homer. The famous Greek doctor, Hippocrates, first used it as a name for the condition 400 years later. His treatment was a mixture of owl's blood in wine.

The first book on asthma was written in 1190 by a Spanish doctor, Moses Maimonides. He believed that attacks of breathlessness could be avoided by a change of climate, less stress, and lots of chicken soup.

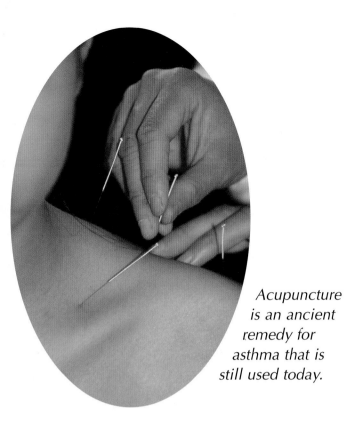

Acupuncture is an ancient remedy for asthma that is still used today.

Discovering triggers

In 1698, an important book called *A Treatise of the Asthma* appeared in England. The author was the first doctor to realize that the weather, dust, infection, and exercise all play a part in asthma.

Modern times

In the 1960s, doctors made a breakthrough and discovered that asthma is caused by inflammation of the airways. Their growing understanding of the way the body reacts to allergens led to today's treatments, which aim to control the inflammation instead of just relaxing the airways.

The future?

Research into asthma is helping to develop better drugs and inhalers, and even new treatments. In the future, it may be possible to immunize people against asthma by injecting them with a **vaccine** against colds or the effects of house dust mites. Another possibility may lie in our **genes** (the "instructions" in our body that are passed on from our parents). Asthma seems to be caused by a faulty gene, which scientists may be able to correct one day.

Scientific research holds out the hope that asthma may be cured one day.

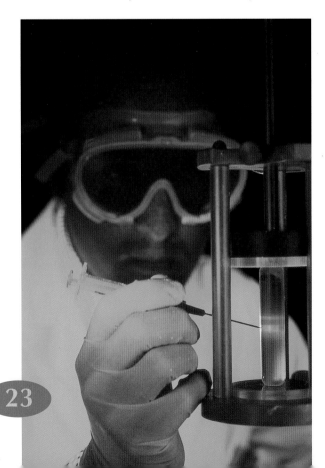

Asthma at school

Most schools have large groups of pupils with asthma. Most of them are happy and work well, but some may have problems. How can schools support them?

Noticing problems
Many children with asthma lead full lives at school. But sometimes their asthma may worsen, and they will have sleepless nights, miss gym, or have to take days off. They may fall behind in classes or feel left out.

Test stress
For older children, school can be part of the problem. When they are preparing for tests, stress may make their symptoms worse. They need extra support at these times.

How can schools help?
Teachers need to know about asthma medicines and be confident about dealing with an attack. They should make the school as asthma-friendly as possible. Teachers need to make sure that every pupil, even those without asthma, understands the condition. Everyone should be helpful if someone has an attack.

Did you know?

- Some children with asthma miss more than one month from school every year.
- Many children with asthma are embarrassed about using their inhaler at school.
- Singing or playing a wind instrument can help people with asthma to improve their breathing.

The American Lung Association encourages schools to let children carry their rescue meds. The Association is also trying to get schools to:

- Have an action plan on file for each child with asthma, noting the medicines that he or she takes.
- Make sure all staff know what to do in an asthma attack.
- Make sure children with asthma take part fully in school life, including gym.
- Keep in touch with parents, and inform them about any asthma attack.
- Encourage other children to understand asthma.

Children with asthma can play and exercise like anyone else.

Physical education

Schools should encourage every pupil to take part in gym. Exercise is important for everyone, including children with asthma. If exercise triggers a pupil's asthma symptoms, they should take a couple of puffs of their rescue med a few minutes before the start of the class and be sure to warm-up first. The inhaler should always be close at hand.

Playing a wind instrument can help children to blow harder and may improve the condition of their lungs.

Asthma at home

Asthma can affect family life in all sorts of ways. For example, tiles on the floor and shades at the windows may be signs that someone in the house has asthma.

Down with dust

The major trigger for asthma in the home is the house dust mite. Even in clean houses there is an enormous amount of dust, mostly from flakes of dead skin that brush off the people who live there. Dust mites feed on dust in carpets, curtains, and furniture. They like to hide in warm, stuffy places in bedrooms and living rooms.

Sleeping in the top bunk rather than the bottom bunk is better for children with asthma.

Hard floors and shades

Replacing carpets with hard flooring and curtains with shades cuts down the places where mites can live. Opening windows to air rooms, dusting with a damp cloth, and vacuuming daily can cut the number of mites by half.

Homes where someone has asthma need to be kept dust-free.

Beds and bunks

When someone has asthma, it's best to keep their bedroom uncluttered. Cutting down on soft toys gives mites fewer places to hide. Special covers on mattresses, comforters, and pillows help to kill mites. Bed linen should be washed every week, and pillows and blankets once a month.

If children sleep in bunk beds, those in the bottom bunk are more likely to have asthma symptoms than those on top. This is because they breathe in the allergens from their own mattress as well as the one above.

No pets

Pets are such a common trigger that many families decide against one. This can be a disappointment for everyone.

Many animals are triggers for people with asthma, but it can be tough not to have a pet.

Some children may need to avoid felt-tip pens if the fumes irritate their airways.

No smoking

Because smoke lingers in the air and drifts from room to room, many families where someone has asthma have a no-smoking rule.

An extra strain

Sometimes asthma can put a strain on the family. There may be times when a child with asthma has extra attention. This can make brothers and sisters feel jealous.

"When I came back from the hospital, my sister liked all the attention I was getting. She kept doing fake coughs and saying 'I've got asthma. I've got asthma.'"

ALISON, AGE 8

Questions people ask

I'm worried I will have asthma for ever. Will I grow out of it?
Only about one in three children lose their asthma completely as they grow older. Some children find their asthma gets better during the teenage years, but it can come back in later life.

Is there a cure for asthma?
Not yet, but scientists are working hard on the problem. Their work will help us to understand much more about how and why asthma develops. Meanwhile, new and better medicines are becoming available all the time.

The warm, moist air in a swimming pool rarely bothers people with asthma.

I love sport, but I have asthma. Are there any sports that help people with asthma? Are there any that I should avoid?
Team sports are good because they can give you the chance to rest and get your breath back. Indoor swimming rarely brings on symptoms unless the water is very cold or contains a lot of chlorine. Sports, such as indoor basketball and hockey are good in winter. Sports you should avoid include scuba diving, climbing, hiking, or skiing.

Team sports can offer chances to rest.

I'm frightened my friend may have an asthma attack. Is it true that you can die from asthma?

There are deaths from asthma, but they are extremely rare and becoming rarer. Better treatments for asthma now mean that most people can control their asthma. Meanwhile, the best way you can help your friend is to know exactly what to do in an asthma attack. Have a look at the advice on page 13.

When are children old enough to carry and use their own rescue meds?

By the age of seven, most children are old enough to carry their own rescue med and decide when to use it. If they are younger than this and at school, they should be able to reach it right away.

By the age of seven, most children are old enough to carry their own rescue med.

Are there any jobs that I wouldn't be able to do?

You should think carefully before applying for jobs that involve close contact with asthma triggers, such as animals, dust, sprays, chemicals, and fumes. There is no list of jobs you can't do—but you might not pass the health test for some jobs.

Teachers must make sure that young children have inhalers nearby at all times.

Glossary

acupuncture A Chinese healing method that works by putting fine needles into parts of the body.

airway A tube that carries air from the windpipe into the lungs. Airways become smaller as they go deeper into the lungs.

allergen A substance that causes the body to react badly. Nuts, milk, seafood, wheat, pollen, cats, dogs, and house dust mites are the common allergens for people with asthma.

allergy A person's sensitivity to something (an allergen) that may not harm other people. It may cause asthma, eczema, sneezing attacks, or other problems.

bronchiole A small airway in the lungs.

dose The amount of medicine given to a patient.

eczema A disease in which the skin is red, itchy, and crusty on parts of the body.

fungus (plural fungi) An organism that is neither an animal nor a plant, such as mold or a mushroom.

gene A unit in the body with information that makes us look or behave in a special way. Genes are found in every cell and are inherited from parents.

hayfever An allergic reaction to pollen and dust. It causes sneezing, a runny nose, and watery eyes.

immunization Giving someone a vaccine that will protect them from a particular disease.

inflamed Hot, red, sore, and swollen. An inflammation is the hot, sore swelling that results from an injury or infection in a part of the body.

inhaler A small plastic device that delivers asthma medicine.

lung One of the two sponge-like organs in your chest that fill with air when you breathe in.

meditation Thinking deeply in order to feel calm, peaceful, and relaxed.

microscopic Too small to be seen with the naked eye.

moisturize To make less dry.

mucus A slimy fluid which protects the linings of your mouth, nose, airways, and digestive tubes.

nebulizer A machine that turns liquid medicine into a mist which can then be breathed deeply into the lungs.

occupational To do with work.

particle A tiny fragment of material, such as a speck of dust.

peak flow meter A plastic tube that shows how well your lungs are working by measuring how hard you can blow out.

preventer An asthma medicine that soothes the airways and makes an asthma attack less likely.

reliever An asthma medicine that relaxes the muscles in the airways, making it easier to breathe.

spacer A clear plastic device that is fixed to an inhaler. It helps asthma medicine to reach the airways.

symptom One of the effects shown or felt by a person who has a disease. For example, coughing is a symptom of asthma.

trigger Something that causes the symptoms of an allergy to appear.

vaccine A substance that is given to a person to protect them against a disease.

weep To ooze liquid.

wheezing Breathing noisily and with difficulty.

windpipe The tube that links the throat to the lungs.

yoga A type of exercise that stretches the body. It can help people to relax and improves the way they breathe.

Useful organizations

Here are some organizations you can contact for more information about asthma.

Asthma and Allergy Foundation
  of America (AAFA)
1233 20th St, NW, Suite 402
Washington D.C. 20036

Tel: (202) 727 8462
email: info@aafa.org

American Lung Association
1740 Broadway
New York 10019

Tel: (212) 315 8700
email: info@lungusa.org

Allergy and Asthma Network
2751 Prosperity Avenue, Suite 150
Fairfax, VA 22031

Tel: (800) 878 4403

Index

acupuncture 22, 23, 30
air pollution 9, 10, 16
airways 6–7, 10, 14, 15,
    16, 23, 27, 30
allergens 7, 9, 20, 23,
    27, 30
allergy 6, 20, 30
animals 7, 11, 16, 20,
    21, 25, 27, 29
asthma attack 5, 7, 10,
    12–13, 15, 24
asthma nurse 12, 18–19,
    29

breathlessness 4, 5, 7, 9,
    10, 12, 22
bunk beds 26, 27

cigarettes 10, 11, 16,
    25, 27
cleaning 10, 16, 26
colds & flu 9, 10, 16, 23
controllers 14–15, 31
controlling asthma 7,
    14–17, 18, 23, 29
coughing 5, 7, 10, 12, 13
cure for asthma 23, 28

diary 16, 17
diet 16
doctors 8, 13, 18, 22, 23
dust mites 10, 16, 21,
    23, 26, 27

eczema 8, 20–21, 30
exercise 5, 10, 14, 17,
    23, 25, 28

fungi 11, 30

genes 23, 30
growing out of asthma
    8, 9, 28

hayfever 8, 30
Hippocrates 22
hospital 12, 13

immunization 9, 23, 30
inhaler 14–15, 18, 23,
    24, 25, 30

lungs 4, 5, 6–7, 13, 14,
    16, 17, 25, 30

medicine 7, 11, 12, 13,
    14–15, 17, 18, 19, 25,
    28
mucus 6, 7, 31

nebulizer 12–13, 31

occupational asthma 9,
    31

peak flow meter 17, 18,
    19, 31

pets see animals
pollen 7, 11, 17, 20, 21

relievers 14–15, 31
rescue meds 13, 14, 15,
    17, 25, 29

school 24–25, 29
scientists 9, 23, 28
sleeping 5, 13, 18, 21,
    24, 26
smoke see cigarettes
soft toys 10, 27
spacer 15, 19, 31
sport see exercise
spray paints 9, 10, 29
stress 22, 24
symptoms of asthma 4,
    5, 7, 8, 10, 11, 12–13,
    14, 17, 24, 27, 28, 31

triggers 7, 9, 10–11, 13,
    16, 17, 20, 25, 26, 27,
    29, 31

washing 16, 17, 27
weather 7, 10, 11, 16,
    21, 23
wheezing 5, 7, 8, 12, 31
windpipe 6, 31

yoga 17, 22, 31